DEER RIDGE ELEM

W9-BEQ-337

30071001103121   B HUDGENS
Vanessa Hudgens

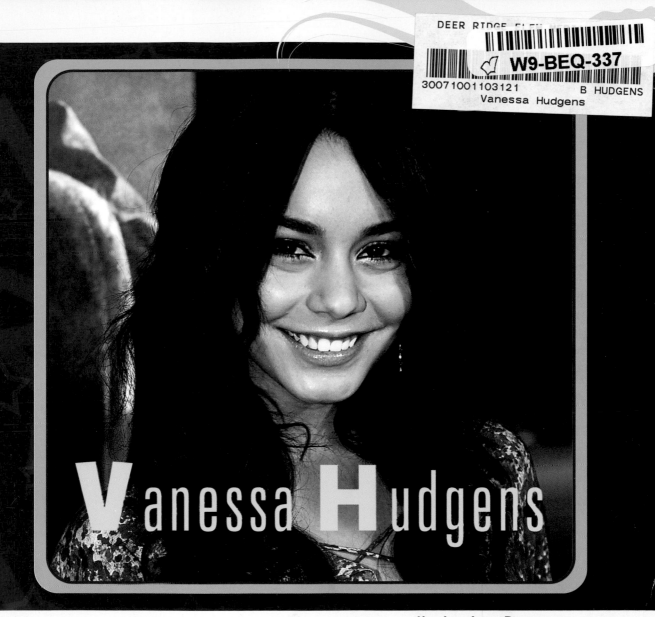

Vanessa Hudgens

Katherine Rawson

PowerKiDS
press.

New York

Published in 2010 by The Rosen Publishing Group, Inc.
29 East 21st Street, New York, NY 10010

Copyright © 2010 by The Rosen Publishing Group, Inc.

All rights reserved. No part of this book may be reproduced in any form without permission in writing from the publisher, except by a reviewer.

First Edition

Editor: Nicole Pristash
Book Design: Kate Laczynski
Book Layout: Julio Gil
Photo Researcher: Jessica Gerweck

Photo Credits: Cover Gabriel Bouys/AFP/Getty Images; p. 4 Vera Anderson/WireImage/Getty Images; p. 7 Jordan Strauss/WireImage/Getty Images; p. 8 © Ning Chiu/ZUMA/Corbis; p. 11 Duval/FilmMagic/Getty Images; p. 12 Kevin Kane/WireImage/Getty Images; p. 15 Tim Mosenfelder/Getty Images; p. 16 David Livingston/Getty Images; p. 19 Victor Chavez/WireImage/Getty Images; p. 20 Mark Sullivan/WireImage for Elizabeth Glaser Pediatric AIDS/Getty Images.

Library of Congress Cataloging-in-Publication Data

Rawson, Katherine.
  Vanessa Hudgens / Katherine Rawson. — 1st ed.
     p. cm. — (Kid stars!)
  Includes index.
  ISBN 978-1-4042-8137-0 (library binding) — ISBN 978-1-4358-3408-8 (pbk.) —
ISBN 978-1-4358-3409-5 (6-pack)
  1. Hudgens, Vanessa, 1988– —Juvenile literature. 2. Actors—United States—Biography—Juvenile literature. 3. Singers—United States—Biography—Juvenile literature. I. Title.
  PN2287.H737R39 2010
  91.4302'8092—dc22
  [B]
                                          2009009587

Manufactured in the United States of America

Contents

Vanessa is a talented actress and singer. Many believe that she will have a lot of success in Hollywood.

Meet Vanessa Hudgens

Vanessa Hudgens is one of the brightest young stars in Hollywood. She first became famous for her sweet smile when she played Gabriella Montez in *High School Musical*. Today, she is a star!

Vanessa is a young woman with many talents. She has acted both in movies and on TV. Vanessa also sings. She has recorded songs for *High School Musical* and has made two albums of her own. Her fans love to watch her act, and they enjoy listening to her music. Do you want to know more about Vanessa? Here's a look at the life of this **popular** new star!

A Talented Family

Vanessa Anne Hudgens was born on December 14, 1988, in Salinas, California. Her mother and father are Gina and Greg Hudgens. Vanessa is not the only talented member of her family. Her younger sister, Stella, is also an actress, and Vanessa's grandmother and grandfather were **musicians**.

When Vanessa was young, she took music and dance classes. Her first acting and singing roles were in community theater **productions** of *The Wizard of Oz* and *Cinderella*. Vanessa was just eight years old when she started acting. Soon, Vanessa began to audition, or try out, for parts on TV and in movies.

Vanessa's sister Stella Hudgens (left) has appeared on the TV show *According to Jim* and in the movie *The Memory Thief*.

Here Vanessa is shown at the premiere, or first showing, of *Thunderbirds* in California. Vanessa said that playing the character Tin-Tin was a lot of fun.

Hard at Work

Vanessa worked hard trying out for roles, or parts. Her hard work paid off. She appeared on the TV show *Still Standing* in 2002 and *The Brothers Garcia* in 2003. Then, she got a part in the movie *Thirteen*. This was Vanessa's first movie role. She played a girl named Noel, who is a friend of the main character.

Vanessa did not stop there. In 2004, she appeared in the movie *Thunderbirds*, as a character named Tin-Tin. Vanessa was working and getting parts, but soon her life would change completely. In 2005, when she was 17, Vanessa got her biggest role yet.

High School Musical

Vanessa played the role of Gabriella Montez in the 2006 Disney movie *High School Musical*. In the movie, Gabriella is one of the smartest girls at East High. She likes Troy, a boy who plays on their school's basketball team. Gabriella and Troy decide to audition for the school's winter musical, against their friends' wishes. When their spoiled classmate Sharpay Evans tries to stop them, though, their friends come together to help them out. In the end, the students learn to get along.

Vanessa and the other actors worked hard to make the movie. Vanessa became good friends with the other members of the cast.

After *High School Musical* came out, Vanessa (center) and her cast mates traveled to other countries. Here they are shown at the movie's premiere in England on September 10, 2006.

Vanessa has said that singing and making music is something she has wanted to do for a long time. She says that dancing to her own music is a dream come true for her.

Her Own Music

High School Musical was one of the most popular TV movies of 2006. More than seven **million** people watched it the first night that it aired on TV. The **sound track** from the movie was the best-selling album of the year.

Vanessa enjoyed singing songs from *High School Musical* so much that she decided to record an album of her own. She worked very hard, and she finished it in just two months. Vanessa's first album is called *V*, and it was **released** in September 2006. *V* went gold. That means at least 500,000 **copies** of the album were sold!

On Tour

By fall 2006, Vanessa was very busy. In October and November, she went on tour with The Cheetah Girls. The Cheetah Girls is a female musical group. A group on tour plays **concerts** around the country. Then, throughout the winter, the cast members from *High School Musical* went on tour. Millions of kids got to see the cast sing songs from *High School Musical* in person.

"Touring is **tough**," Vanessa has said. Touring might be hard work, but it is an important part of Vanessa's job as a singer. Touring allows Vanessa to share her music with people across the country.

While on tour, Vanessa (center) and the *High School Musical* cast played concerts in more than 40 cities in the United States and Latin America. This is a concert in San Jose, California.

In November 2007, the *High School Musical 2* sound track won an American Music Award. This picture shows Vanessa (second from right) and the cast at the award show.

More High School

Since *High School Musical* was so popular, Disney decided to make a second movie. In *High School Musical 2*, Gabriella, Troy, and their friends get summer jobs at Sharpay's country club. Gabriella must deal with Troy as he learns to be true to himself and his friends as they put on a talent show. The movie first appeared on TV in August 2007. More than 17 million people watched it!

Vanessa had become very famous, and several companies wanted her to be in **commercials** for their products. Vanessa has done commercials for Neutrogena beauty products and Echo Red shoes.

Back on the Road

Even though Vanessa was acting a lot, she continued to sing as well. In July 2008, Vanessa released her second album, *Identified*. The album sold more than 22,000 copies in its first week. "Sneakernight" is one of the songs from the album. It became a very popular song to dance to.

During the summer of 2008, Vanessa went on tour again. This tour was called the Identified Summer Tour. Vanessa sang songs from both of her albums at parks and state fairs around the country. She was away from home, but Vanessa got to see her family. Her mother, father, and sister traveled with her.

Vanessa is not only a star in the United States, but she is also famous in Mexico. Here Vanessa is shown singing in Mexico City in September 2008.

Vanessa has said that if it were not for her fans, she would not be where she is today.

What's Next?

Vanessa played Gabriella Montez a third time in *High School Musical 3: Senior Year* in 2008. The movie made $42 million in its first weekend! Vanessa's next movie was another musical, called *Bandslam*. In the movie, she plays a talented musician who plays the guitar and sings.

Vanessa has had a very busy and successful life as a young singer and actor. She hopes for many more successes. "My **passion** is doing movies, and as long as I keep doing that, I'll be happy," Vanessa has said. Her fans look forward to seeing her in more movies and hearing her voice. Vanessa has a bright **future** ahead of her!

VANESSA HUDGENS

 Vanessa has a dog named Shadow.

 Even though Vanessa can sing, she cannot whistle.

 She enjoys going camping when she has time off.

"We're All in This Together" is Vanessa's favorite dance scene from *High School Musical*.

 Science was Vanessa's **favorite** subject in school.

Some of Vanessa's nicknames are Nessa, V, Van, and Vanney.

 She is afraid of heights.

 She likes to listen to rock music.

 Vanessa is best friends with her *High School Musical* costar Ashley Tisdale.

Vanessa's favorite color is red.

Glossary

commercials (kuh-MER-shulz) TV messages that try to sell something.

concerts (KONT-serts) Musical shows.

copies (KO-peez) Things that are made to look and sound exactly the same as something else.

favorite (FAY-vuh-rut) Most liked.

future (FYOO-chur) The time that is coming.

million (MIL-yun) One thousand thousands.

musicians (myoo-ZIH-shunz) People who write, play, or sing music.

passion (PA-shun) A very strong feeling.

popular (PAH-pyuh-lur) Liked by lots of people.

productions (pruh-DUK-shunz) Plays, musicals, TV shows, or movies.

released (rih-LEESD) Put out for sale.

sound track (SOWND TRAK) A music album that goes with a movie or TV show.

tough (TUF) Strong or firm.

Index

A

album(s), 5, 13, 18

C

commercials, 17
concerts, 14
copies, 13, 18

F

fans, 5, 21
future, 21

H

High School Musical, 5, 10, 13–14, 17, 22
Hollywood, 5

M

movie(s), 5–6, 10, 13, 17, 21
musician(s), 6, 21

P

productions, 6

S

science, 22
songs, 5, 13–14, 18
sound track, 13

T

talents, 5
TV, 5–6

Web Sites

Due to the changing nature of Internet links, PowerKids Press has developed an online list of Web sites related to the subject of this book. This site is updated regularly. Please use this link to access the list:
www.powerkidslinks.com/kids/vanessah/